CONTENTS

WELCOME TO DINOSAUR WARS!

Dinosaurs were brutal creatures. They fought each other and ate each other. Usually it was meat-eater versus plant-eater or big versus small. But in Dinosaur Wars, it's a free for all. Plant-eaters attack plant-eaters. Giants fight giants. And small dinosaurs gang up on huge opponents. In Dinosaur Wars, any dinosaur battle is possible!

In this dinosaur war, Spinosaurus and Giganotosaurus battle to the death. You will see how these massive meat-eaters match up. You'll learn about their giant weapons and how they used them in combat. Then you'll see them battling head-to-head – and you'll get to watch from a front row seat!

Spinosaurus (SPINE-oh-sore-us)
Giganotosaurus (gig-an-OH-toe-sore-us)

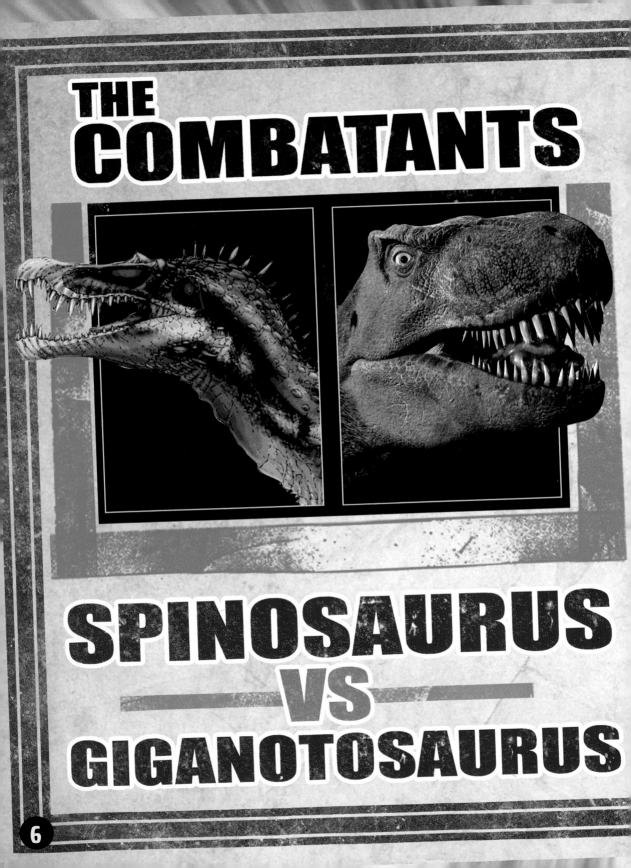

THE COMBATANTS

SPINOSAURUS
VS
GIGANOTOSAURUS

Spinosaurus and Giganotosaurus never actually fought. Spinosaurus lived on the northern coast of Africa. Meanwhile, Giganotosaurus lived at the southern tip of South America.

Still, before they became **extinct**, they did share the earth for 5 million years. Giganotosaurus survived for 22 million years, from about 112 to 90 million years ago. Spinosaurus lived from about 95 to 70 million years ago.

These were two of the largest **predators** ever to walk the earth. They probably wouldn't have hunted each other. However, if they had lived in the same area, they may have fought over a meal. After all, they were both so big that they had to eat a lot of food.

Tyrannosaurus rex was once thought to be the largest land predator ever. But both Spinosaurus and Giganotosaurus were longer and heavier than T. rex. They are the largest known land predators of all time.

FIERCE FACT
BIGGEST PREDATORS

extinct no longer living anywhere in the world
predator animal that hunts other animals for food

SIZE

Spinosaurus
18 metres long; 8.2 tonnes
★ ★ ★ ★ ★

★ ★ ★ ★ ★
Giganotosaurus
12 metres long; 7.7 tonnes

Spinosaurus was up to 18 metres (59 feet) long from head to tail. That's about the same length as a bendy bus. Spinosaurus' head measured almost 1.8 metres (6 feet) long. He had a spiny sail on his back, similar to the back fins of many fish. The sail stood more than 1.8 metres (6 feet) high at the tallest point. Spinosaurus weighed more than 8.2 tonnes. He had the size and strength to overpower almost anything that got in his way.

Spinosaurus' sail was probably used to identify others of its own kind. It may have also made him look larger than he really was to scare off other dinosaurs.

FIERCE FACT
THE SAIL

Giganotosaurus was one of the few creatures in history that could match Spinosaurus in size. At around 12 metres (39 feet) long, Giganotosaurus was shorter than Spinosaurus. But what Giganotosaurus lacked in length, he made up for in weight. He tipped the scales at about 7.7 tonnes. Although he was slightly smaller than Spinosaurus, Giganotosaurus would still be tough to beat in a fight.

SPEED AND AGILITY

Giganotosaurus had strong back legs and probably ran fast for short distances. But with his stockier frame, it is unlikely he could stop or turn quickly. Giganotosaurus probably hunted giant long-necked dinosaurs that didn't move quickly. He didn't need to be fast to be a successful hunter.

Spinosaurus was sleeker and more streamlined than the stocky Giganotosaurus. He could probably move quickly on land. But Spinosaurus had a bigger advantage in the water, where he hunted for most of his food. With his streamlined body, he could wade into deep water and still move quickly. Spinosaurus' quickness would be a big advantage in a fight.

SPINOSAURUS' WEAPONS

Spinosaurus had a long, flat snout like a crocodile. His long jaws were full of huge, deadly teeth. But unlike most **carnivores**, Spinosaurus had teeth that were spaced fairly far apart. They were straight, smooth, and cone-shaped. They were made for stabbing through meat rather than slicing it. Scientists think his teeth and jaws were made for catching fish instead of killing large **prey** on land.

FIERCE FACT

DESTROYED FOSSILS

The first Spinosaurus fossils ever discovered were destroyed in a bombing raid in Germany during World War II (1939–1945). No other Spinosaurus fossils were found until the 1980s.

Like many other predators, Spinosaurus had three clawed fingers on each hand. But while many large meat-eaters had very short arms, Spinosaurus' arms were much longer. Being able to reach further may have given him an advantage against Giganotosaurus.

carnivore animal that eats only meat
prey animal that is hunted by other animals

GIGANOTOSAURUS' WEAPONS

At 20 centimetres (8 inches) long, Giganotosaurus' teeth were enormous. They were flat like a shark's teeth, but they were longer and narrower. They were **serrated** like a knife blade to slice through flesh and cause a lot of bleeding.

If Giganotosaurus got hold of his enemies, they were in trouble. Although he was a little smaller than Spinosaurus, his jaws were much more powerful. His superior bite strength would be a huge advantage in any fight.

serrated having a jagged edge

14

Giganotosaurus also had sharp claws
on each of his six fingers. He could use
these curved claws for slashing an enemy
or gripping his prey.

ATTACK STYLE

Spinosaurus
Nimble slasher

★ ★ ★ ★ ★

★ ★ ★ ★ ★

Giganotosaurus
Ferocious biter

Spinosaurus was built to hunt in the water and on land. Evidence shows that he ate fish and other dinosaurs. His long snout and unique teeth were made to grab and hang on to wildly squirming prey. With his long arms, he could stab at fish in the water or grab a victim on land. His neck was longer than the necks of most large meat-eaters. It allowed him to quickly dart his head forward to grab prey. In a fight, his long neck would provide a reach advantage against Giganotosaurus.

Spinosaurus' nostrils sat fairly high up on his snout. This feature allowed him to keep part of his snout underwater while still breathing.

FIERCE FACT
THE SNOUT

Some scientists think Giganotosaurus hunted in packs. It might seem unnecessary for such a large predator, but hunting in packs would have helped bring down huge prey. Giganotosaurus probably hunted mighty **herbivores** like Argentinosaurus, which weighed about 90 tonnes. A pack of Giganotosaurus probably bit their prey again and again. Each bite would tear away chunks of flesh until the victim bled to death.

GET READY TO RUMBLE!

Are you ready for the main event? Two giant meat-eaters are out to prove who's the biggest, most dangerous beast of the prehistoric world. In one corner is the fierce hunter – Spinosaurus! He's big, he's tough, and he's mean. In the other corner is his opponent – Giganotosaurus! His name says it all. He's gigantic, deadly, and hungry. Nobody can guess which of these super-sized dinosaurs will win this fight. But one thing is certain – the winner will be bloody, battered, and bruised!

You've got a front row seat. So sit back, turn the page, and get ready to enjoy the battle!

SPINOSAURUS

SIZE ★★★★★ ★★★★

SPEED AND AGILITY ★★★ ★★

WEAPONS ★★★★★ ★★★★

ATTACK STYLE ★★★★★ ★★★★

GIGANOTOSAURUS

ONE LAST THING...

This battle is make-believe. Like Goldilocks and the three bears – it never happened. Even scientists don't know everything about these two mighty dinosaurs. But we do know they were big, mean, and hungry – and they could fight. This should be one gigantic good show!

THE BATTLE

Spinosaurus splashes through the ocean. He cranes his neck low and scans the water. Just beyond him, stormy waves crash down. Foamy water rumbles towards the shore. Neither the rain nor the violent sea seems to bother the monstrous Spinosaurus.

Suddenly, he plunges his long snout into the salty water. His jaws snap shut. Below the surface, his teeth bite into the tail of a long, brown fish. He jerks his snout upward to pull the fish from the water. The fish thrashes wildly and begins to slip from his grasp.

The hungry beast clamps his mouth tight to get a better grip. But the fish slips and splashes into the sea. Spinosaurus swipes his clawed hand through the water to grab the big fish. Then he flips it into the air and catches it in his toothy jaws.

He holds the struggling fish tightly in his jaws and turns towards the shore. There he spots Giganotosaurus.

Fossils show that some fish living at the same time as Spinosaurus grew up to 6 metres (20 feet) long. These fish would have made a decent meal for even the largest Spinosaurus.

FIERCE FACT
BIG MEAL

Giganotosaurus has been watching Spinosaurus splashing in the water. The giant meat-eater sees the huge fish hanging from Spinosaurus' mouth. He suddenly feels hungry.

Giganotosaurus stomps into the water and heads straight for Spinosaurus. He quickly reaches his opponent. He roars and thrusts his massive head forward. He snaps his jaws shut on the fish.

Spinosaurus tries to jerk the fish away, but Giganotosaurus holds on tightly. The two giant predators tug again. Suddenly, the fish breaks apart. Giganotosaurus stumbles deeper into the water. He's already lost his balance when a towering wave slams against him. He plunges into the dark sea.

Giganotosaurus means "giant southern lizard".

FIERCE FACT

NAME

Giganotosaurus crashes into the wet sand beneath the water. He lifts his head and climbs to his feet. But Spinosaurus is waiting for him. He snaps his long jaws around Giganotosaurus' neck.

Giganotosaurus roars. Spinosaurus holds on tight. He tugs his opponent further into the water. Giganotosaurus stumbles and falls to his knees. Spinosaurus forces his enemy's head below the dark waves. He leans his massive body weight against his foe to hold him under the water.

Giganotosaurus tries to roar. But his mouth fills with salty water. He begins to panic. He finds the sandy bottom with his feet and pushes up with all his strength. He rises wildly out of the foamy water. But Spinosaurus is still gripping his neck. The two giant dinosaurs topple sideways and crash into the stormy sea.

FIERCE FACT

NAME

Spinosaurus means "spine lizard".

Giganotosaurus climbs to his feet first. Spinosaurus still clings to his enemy's neck. Giganotosaurus jerks his head back and forth. He flops like a fish trying to break free from Spinosaurus' grip. Dark blood seeps from Giganotosaurus' neck and streams into the water.

Spinosaurus finally finds his footing and tugs back on Giganotosaurus. Giganotosaurus roars and slashes at Spinosaurus with his clawed hand. But his arm is too short. His swing misses his huge opponent.

A giant wave suddenly crashes into the two monsters. Spinosaurus loses his footing, but he still hangs on to his enemy. Giganotosaurus charges out of the water and onto the beach, dragging Spinosaurus with him.

Spinosaurus' weight causes Giganotosaurus to stumble. He falls and crashes down on top of his enemy. Spinosaurus finally loses his grip on Giganotosaurus' neck. Both dinosaurs struggle to climb to their feet.

Spinosaurus rises first. He opens his jaws wide. He darts his head forward to strike. But Giganotosaurus ducks out of the way. He springs forward and clamps his powerful jaws on to Spinosaurus' neck. Spinosaurus shrieks and tries to pull away.

Giganotosaurus twists violently with his powerful neck muscles and massive body. There's a loud snap! Giganotosaurus lets go of Spinosaurus' neck. Spinosaurus flops to the ground. The battle is over.

Giganotosaurus stomps powerfully in the wet sand. He points his huge head towards the stormy sky and bellows a mighty roar. He lets the world know he's just beaten one of the biggest predators ever to walk the earth!

GLOSSARY

carnivore animal that eats only meat

extinct no longer living. An extinct animal is one whose kind has died out completely.

fossil remains or traces of plants and animals that are preserved as rock

herbivore animal that eats only plants

nostril opening in an animal's nose through which it breathes and smells

predator animal that hunts other animals for food

prey animal hunted by another animal for food

serrated having a jagged edge that helps with cutting, such as a saw

stocky having a strong, heavy build

FIND OUT MORE

BOOKS

Dinosaur Encyclopedia, Caroline Bingham (Dorling Kindersley, 2007)

Dinosaur Hunters: Palaeontologists, Louise and Richard Spilsbury (Heinemann Library, 2007)

Prehistoric Scary Creatures, John Malam (Book House, 2008)

WEBSITE

www.nhm.ac.uk/kids-only/dinosaurs
Visit the Natural History Museum's website to discover more than 300 types of dinosaur, play dinosaur games, and find out what sort of dinosaur you would be!

PLACES TO VISIT

Dinosaur Isle
Sandown, Isle of Wight PO36 8QA
www.dinosaurisle.com

Natural History Museum
London SW7 5BD
www.nhm.ac.uk

The Dinosaur Museum
Dorchester DT1 1EW
www.thedinosaurmuseum.com

INDEX